Welcom
Disney Learnin

D0119616

Sharing a book with your child is the perfect opportunity
to cuddle and enjoy the reading experience together.
Research has shown that reading aloud with your child is one
of the most important ways to prepare them for success as a
reader. When you share books together, you help strengthen
your child's reading and vocabulary skills as well as stimulate
their curiosity, imagination and enthusiasm for reading.

In this book, read all about Princess Anna and Queen Elsa.
They are royal sisters, but can they be friends, too? You can
enhance the reading experience by talking to your child
about one of their own experiences with a sibling or a friend.
What are their favourite things about this person? Have they
ever felt misunderstood by the other? Children find it easier
to understand what they read when they can connect it with
their own personal experiences.

Children learn in different ways and at different speeds,
but they all require a supportive environment to nurture a
lifelong love of books, reading and learning. The *Adventures
in Reading* books are carefully levelled to present new
challenges to developing readers, and are filled with familiar
and fun characters from the wonderful world of Disney
to make the learning experience comfortable, positive
and enjoyable.

Enjoy your reading adventure together!

For Lilly and Lucy, the sweetest sisters
– M.L.

Scholastic Children's Books
Euston House,
24 Eversholt Street,
London NW1 1DB, UK

A division of Scholastic Ltd
London • New York • Toronto • Sydney • Auckland
Mexico City • New Delhi • Hong Kong

This book was first published in the United States by Random House Children's Books in 2013.
Published in Australia in 2014 by Scholastic Australia.
This edition published in the UK by Scholastic Ltd in 2015.

ISBN 978 1 4071 6298 0

Printed in Malaysia

2 4 6 8 10 9 7 5 3 1

www.scholastic.co.uk

A Tale of
Two Sisters

ADVENTURES IN READING

By Melissa Lagonegro
Illustrated by Maria Elena Naggi, Studio IBOIX and
the Disney Storybook Artists

Elsa and Anna were sisters. Elsa
was older. Anna was younger.

Elsa had a secret magic power.
She could create ice and snow!

One day, Elsa and Anna were playing.
Elsa made a mistake. Her magic hit
Anna by accident.

Anna got very sick and cold.
Their parents were very worried.
Elsa was very frightened.

The King and Queen took Anna
to the trolls. An old troll helped
Anna get better.

Anna wanted to be friends with Elsa.
But Elsa stayed away from her.
She wanted to keep Anna safe.

Anna and Elsa grew up. Anna met Prince Hans. They fell in love straight away.

Elsa became queen. But she could not
tell anyone about her magical secret.

Anna wanted to marry Hans.
But Elsa did not agree with her sister.
She wanted Anna to wait.

Anna and Elsa argued. Anna pulled off Elsa's glove. Magical ice shot from Elsa's hand!

Everyone knew Elsa's secret!
But Elsa did not want to hurt
anyone, so she ran far away.

Elsa built an ice palace in the mountains. The land was covered with ice and snow.

Now the kingdom was in trouble. There was too much snow! Anna wanted to find Elsa and bring her home.

She met Kristoff and his reindeer, Sven. They helped her search for Elsa.

They met a snowman called Olaf.
Elsa had made him with her magic
powers. Olaf led them to Elsa.

Back at the castle,
Hans was worried
about Anna. He
wanted to find her.

Anna went to Elsa's ice palace.
She told Elsa about the snow.
She asked her to come home.

Elsa was too scared. She did not want to hurt anyone. But Anna would not leave without Elsa.

Elsa got very angry. She blasted Anna with ice. It hit Anna in her heart by mistake.

Kristoff and Olaf took Anna away.
She was getting very sick again.

Elsa's magic was turning Anna to ice!
Kristoff took Anna to see the trolls.
But the old troll could not help her.

Only an act of true love
could save Anna now.

Hans had gone to the mountains.
He found Elsa. His guards brought
her back to the castle.

Anna went back to the castle.
But Hans would not save her.
He did not really love her at all.

Kristoff did love Anna. He rushed to save her. But then Anna saw that Hans was going to hurt Elsa.

Anna ran to save her sister.
She blocked Hans's sword.
She froze into solid ice.

Elsa was very sad. She cried and hugged her frozen sister. Then something magical happened!

Anna began to melt. She loved her sister so much that the spell was broken!

Anna and Elsa were not
just sisters. Now they were
best friends as well!